About the Author

Hilary was born on 4 March 1964 in Yorkshire. Her parents lived in Thornton Dale. After the family was complete with her sister, the whole family, including two beagles, eventually settled in Derby. She qualified as an Enrolled Nurse in October 1986, and nursed in various locations around England. Having qualified as a Staff Nurse in 1992, she was in nursing for over 37 years.

Hilary had to retire recently on health grounds, and is now enjoying pursuing her hobbies which include reading, craft work and music. She is currently organist at her local church, and is also working towards her music exams in classical organ.

Hilary initially wrote this book soon after her mother died, as it helped her with the grieving process. Since she first started it her father has also passed away, and she eventually decided to see about publishing the book, to help others in their journey.

Hilary is married and lives with her lovely husband and a collie called Lightning.

*Dedicated to Mum
and Dad
who always saw a little of heaven
in nature around them
and had a very quiet, strong faith.*

*No person is ever truly alone.
Those who live no more
whom we loved,
echo still within our thoughts.*

*Our words, our hearts and
what they did and who they are
become a part of all that we are forever.*

Hilary Goodman

REFLECTIONS

AUSTIN MACAULEY PUBLISHERS™
LONDON • CAMBRIDGE • NEW YORK • SHARJAH

Original text copyright © Hilary Goodman 2023
Selection copyright © Hilary Goodman 2023

The right of Hilary Goodman to be identified as author and compiler of this work has been asserted in accordance with sections 77 and 78 of the Copyright, Designs and Patents Act 1988.

All rights reserved. No part of this publication may be reproduced, stored in a retrieval system, or transmitted in any form or by any means, electronic, mechanical, photocopying, recording, or otherwise, without the prior permission of the publishers.

Any person who commits any unauthorised act in relation to this publication may be liable to criminal prosecution and civil claims for damages.

Following efforts to trace copyright holders and to obtain their permission for the use of copyright material, the publisher apologises for any outstanding omissions and would be grateful to be notified of corrections that should be incorporated in future reprints.

A CIP catalogue record for this title is available from the British Library.

All photographs by Paul Goodman.

ISBN 9781528955065 (Paperback)
ISBN 9781398449480 (ePub e-book)

www.austinmacauley.com

First published 2023
Austin Macauley Publishers Ltd
1 Canada Square
Canary Wharf
London
E14 5AA

Contents

Introduction: My Experience 9

Synopsis of Sections 12

Poems & Sayings 15

Haikus 29

Prayers & Thoughts 35

Hymns & Psalms 43

Talks 55

INTRODUCTION: MY EXPERIENCE

I have been nursing for over 37 years, beginning as a nursing assistant in an Elderly Nursing Home in Derby. During that time, I found that I had a vocation, and after several interviews settled on doing my Pupil Nurse training, that would lead to an Enrolled Nurse (EN) qualification. I qualified as an EN in 1986, and found myself away from home in Macclesfield. After a tumultuous start, I found my bearings, and my strong religious faith kept me going. I would go to my local Christian bookshop and sit and read the Bible whilst having a coffee. It was during these times that I became immersed in the teachings of Jesus; I particularly loved reading the parables.

On my return to Derby, I quickly found that I was becoming restless, so I was on the move again. This time to Northamptonshire, to a rehabilitation unit, where I met my future husband. I was fortunate to gain access to the conversion course, which allowed me to change from an EN to a Registered Mental Health Nurse (RMN). This I achieved in a year, after which we got married.

I have had a variety of jobs throughout my nursing life, each with their own challenges. I have been deputy manager of a nursing home, twice. I have worked with clients who have learning disabilities. Some clients have challenging, some profound and some elderly, and I have seen the difficulties that they face. I have also been a staff nurse. Throughout this time there were occasions when I came face to face with death, either by being present as the person was dying, or while laying the body out for the relatives. I know that after a while you can become accustomed to it, but I would still shed a tear when they left the nursing home with the undertakers.

When Mum died, I was at the time a deputy manager and felt I had to put on a brave face for the family's sake. I helped Dad with sorting out the funeral directors, the registering of the death, the organising of the service: throughout that time, I didn't feel able to show any weakness, but the church and my faith kept me going. I would sit and read the Bible and take comfort from the words.

When Dad died, I experienced was a different set of emotions. He died in hospital, and because it was a sudden death, it had to go to the coroner. I went away for a week to get my head round it; on my return, I helped my sister with the funeral arrangements, the registering of the death, all the practical issues that surround the passing of someone who is well loved. I did shed tears when Dad died, particularly when he went into the church prior to the funeral service on Christmas Eve. Again, my strong faith kept me going throughout the day.

The initial idea of writing and reflecting was to help me through the darkest days following my mum's death. It was difficult at times to see past the upheaval that death can cause; even five years later, when Dad passed away, it still seemed hard to process.

Through the whole process of losing both parents, the strong faith that they instilled in me from an early age never faltered; in fact, in many ways it has deepened my faith.

These may be personal reflections, but there are chapters and individual pieces within the book that I hope will touch you and inspire you on your journey. Whatever you are going through, please rest assured that you are not on your own: there is always someone you can turn to.

I hope that you will find the peace and comfort from reading and reflecting, as I have found peace and comfort in writing this book.

Yours in Christ

Hilary

SYNOPSIS OF SECTIONS

POEMS & SAYINGS

This chapter incorporates a variety of poems and short sentences, some well known and others not so, that I have found to be thought-provoking as well as comforting.

PRAYERS & THOUGHTS

These include prayers from a variety of sources, including a few thoughts for Advent, to encourage people to stop and take note.

As I say, I enjoy talking to my heavenly Father, as much as I enjoyed talking to my earthly father.

HYMNS & PSALMS

'How sweet the name of Jesus sounds' is important to me as it speaks of Jesus as a friend, brother, comforter, priest and king, no matter where you are in your life, this hymn will speak to you.

'I heard the voice of Jesus say' speaks of Jesus' comforting words, knowing that he will always be there.

I first heard 'Will your anchor hold' when I was on parade as a young Red Cross cadet. We were parading through Derby city centre on the way to a big service at the cathedral.

I found the words reassuring, and didn't realise at the time that it was the Boy's Brigade National Anthem. I wanted it for my wedding song, because it describes married life. It isn't always plain sailing and there can be rough seas, but if you work at it you can pull through and be stronger.

'Eternal Father' was a favourite of my late father's; he was in the Merchant Navy. It was also one of the first hymns that I taught myself to play on the organ. It speaks of the constant reassurance that most of us seek. The tune 'Melita', although difficult to play, reminds me of the sea, with the constant changing of the chords and the accidentals.

'Going Home': we sang this at Mum's funeral, and it is appropriate to include in a book about reflecting. I find the words comforting and reassuring, echoing the memorial acclamation in the Communion Service.

The extracts from the psalms, although short, have helped me through tough times, knowing that there is a short passage that will be relevant at the time.

TALKS

I was approached to take a small morning worship group at church. Being only thirty minutes long, it included three hymns, a talk and prayers. Although daunted by talking in front of people, I enjoyed the preparation and subsequent delivery. The small congregation could hear my passion and my faith coming through.

POEMS & SAYINGS

A SIMPLE POEM

Christ has no body now
on earth but yours
no hands but yours
no feet but yours.

Yours are the eyes
through which He looks
with compassion on
this world.

Yours are the feet with
which He is to go about
doing good
Yours are the hand
with which He is to
bless people now.

St Teresa of Avila (1515–1582)

FOOTPRINTS

One night I had a dream
I was walking along the beach with the Lord.
Across the sky flashed scenes from my life:
for each scene there were two sets of footprints
in the sand, one belonged to me and the other belonged to the Lord.
When the last scene of my life flashed before us, I looked back at the footprints in the sand.
I noticed that at the saddest points in my life, there was only one set of footprints.
I was troubled and I questioned the Lord about it,
'Lord, you said that once I decided to follow you, you would walk with me all the way. But I've noticed during the most troublesome times of my life, there is only one set of footprints. Why when I need you the most did you leave me?'
The Lord replied,
'My precious child, I love you and I would never leave you. During your times of trial and suffering, when you only saw one set of footprints, it was then that I carried you.'

Attributed to Margaret Fishback Powers (1900–1985)

This poem has so much meaning: every time I read it, it continues to inspire me and give me great comfort. The last line has particular meaning.

Do not look forward to what might happen tomorrow, the same everlasting Father who cares for you today will care for you tomorrow and every day.

Either he will shield you from suffering or he will give you unfailing strength to bear it.

Be at peace then and put aside all anxious thoughts and misgivings.

St Francis de Sales (1567–1622)

* * * *

I found God in the morning, we just sat and talked, I kept him near me everywhere I walked.

I called on God at noontime, a heart filled with despair I felt his quiet presence I knew that he was there.

We met again at sunset, the waning of the day I had made him happy I had lived his way.

Then when at bedtime I knelt silently in prayer again his gentle presence, I felt 'someone does care'.

Author unknown

Some poems from a book entitled Quiet Times *by Salesian Missions, that I have found to be helpful in difficult times.*

IN HIS STEPS

Dwell not in the valley of despair,
waste not another day.
Arm yourself with faith and prayer,
and then be on your way.
Yield not unto temptation
which leads the soul astray,
but focus on the light ahead
and walk the narrow way.
Your Guide shall always lead yourself
and shield you from harm's way,
but you must follow in His steps
and listen and obey.
His strength shall never fail yourself
as you stop awhile to pray,
For at the end of your journey
you'll find a brighter day.
At the end of life's journey,
Heaven's just a step away
For all who follow in his steps
and listen and obey.

Clay Harrison

THE LIGHT BEYOND

When somber clouds of steely grey
Cast shadows o'er your heart and way,
Look up, beyond the darkened sky,
Where tints of blue will soon drift by.

Look up and know that in God's plan
No sparrow falls not, too, a man
Without his watch, without his love.
Have faith, believe, trust him, above.

For from the dark is born the light,
A ray of hope, a beacon bright
To warm your heart and help you through.
Rejoice and know God's there with you.

Vi B. Chevalier

GOD'S GIFTS

It's in the silence of the soul,
where peace and wisdom stay,
to guide us through the din and strife,
confronting us each day.

God placed this gift within us,
with his loving Grace,
knowing that we need His love,
when trials of life we face.

This strength will gently guide us,
His love will see us through,
releasing gifts of faith and hop,
to bear, what we must do.

Colette Fedor

TROUBLED WATERS

When I tread on troubled waters
and my faith begins to wane,
with his help I'll rise above it,
He is with me, praise his name.

He will hold my hand in trouble,
He will weep with me in sorrow
and He'll promise that a brighter day
is in store for me tomorrow.

There is no one I can go to
for the comfort he can give,
He will always be there with me
till on earth no more I live.

Then He'll gently lift me upwards
onto his Father's throne,
where pain and heartaches are behind me
in my eternal home.

Albert N. Theel (1929–2003)

The following poems and sayings I found whilst visiting various churches around the country:

THE LOTUS

The beauty and sweet smell of the lotus flower symbolises
man's spiritual growth and evolution.
The roots deep down in muddy water,
represent his lower nature.
The green stem rising up through the water
his intuitive search and growth in wisdom.
And the flower as last blossoming in the sunlight
of self-realisation

Author unknown

* * * *

GOD KNOWS

And I said to the man who stood at the gate of the year:
'Give me a light that I may tread safely into the unknown.'
And he replied:
'Go out into the darkness and put your hand into the Hand of God.
That shall be to you better than light and safer than a known way.'
So I went forth, and finding the Hand of God, trod gladly into the night.
And He led me towards the hills and the breaking of day in the lone East.

Minnie Louise Haskins (1875–1957)

KEEP ON SMILING

It's hard to laugh when things go wrong, it's easy to lose
heart, but if you can keep smiling it's certainly a start.
Happiness seems far away when days are long and sad,
but just as good times pass away
so do all the bad. Trouble always fades away, if you can grin
and bear it. But call me if it gets too much and I'll be there
to share it.

Author unknown

* * * *

God's kindness endureth forever, what
a wonderful thing to know,
when the tides of life run against you
and your spirit is downcast and low.

Helen Steiner Rice (1900–81)

* * * *

Wisdom from God
shows itself most clearly
in a loving heart

Author unknown

* * * *

HOPE, we have this hope as an anchor for the soul
sure and strong.

Author unknown

HOPE IN JESUS

In Jesus your future is secure
and your destiny certain

Roy Lessin

* * * *

Hang on, you can do all things through
Christ who gives you strength.

Author unknown

* * * *

God is in control
when things around you appear dark and terrifying,
hold on the promise of God
He is wholly in control.

Solly Ozrovech (1927–2015)

Time is too slow,
for those who wait.
Too swift,
for those who fear.
Too long,
for those who grieve.
Too short,
for those who rejoice.
But for those who love,
time is eternity.

Henry Van Dyke (1852–1933)

I wrote this when I was feeling low, and I find it very helpful even now:

When I was wandering in the wilderness of pain and torment, I looked up and saw you there.
You were the light shining, beckoning, welcoming, with your arms outstretched.
You picked me up and hugged me, as my own earthly father would.
You wouldn't put me down, until the heavy sobs had turned into gentle tears.
You then said the comforting words,
'I am with you.'

This was written on a memorial card:

You can shed tears
that they have gone.
Or you can smile
because they have lived.

You can close your eyes
and pray that they'll come back
or you can open your eyes
and see all that they have left.

Your heart may be empty
because you don't see them.
Or you can be full of the love
that you have shared.

You can turn your back on tomorrow
and live for yesterday.
Or you can be happy for tomorrow
because of yesterday.

You can remember them
and only that they have gone.
Or you can cherish their memory
and let it live on.

You can cry and close your mind
be empty and turn your back.
Or you can do what they would want
smile, open your eyes, love and go on.

'She is Gone' by David Harkins (b. 1958)

HAIKUS

Poems written in the haiku style, using descriptive words to build up a picture. These are observations of where I have been on holiday. (They are not written in the strict haiku metre of three lines of five, seven and five syllables respectively.)

Gulls screeching overhead
against clear blue sky
waves lap against jetty
wind catches empty masts

Tall houses with view over sea
tall chimneys in regimented rows
gulls land, stand still
cars beneath roll by

Boats on lake gently turn
each one covered, waiting
dingies dart back and forth
gulls bob on water

In far distant train rattles
cars go by, sirens sound
beside the lake a different world
peaceful, quiet, serene and calm

Early morning, dew on ground
squirrels darting through leaves
food clasped in front paws
sitting up taking it all in

Sun glistens on sea like diamonds
waves hit rocks shoots spray
up and over
unsure where it is going

Shutters on shops rattle up
they awake to a dreary cold morning
the high street starts to bustle
people scurrying by

New coffee shop looks inviting
warm and friendly
two ladies in a corner talk about past things
coffee comes steaming hot

Waves crashing onto rocks
white spray leaping up as wave hits
sea retreats back and then
returns bigger and bolder than the last time
I sit on the sea wall watching

Tall trees that tower over everything
ever reaching with their branches to the sky
imposing as they stand in line
rank on rank as though
waiting for some command

The ducks make such a racket
amidst the tranquility of the lake
the soft wind blows across the lake
leaving little ripples of chaos

The fish hide in the shadows
darting to and fro
yet don't seem bothered
when the ducks go through them

The strange rocky outcrops
stand precariously on the top of the moors
unsure of how they got there

Sun sets amidst pink clouds
heralding the evening
moon shine in a dark sky
too early for stars to come out

The birds around the site sing their final song
before they go
the gulls remain noisy
calling to one another

The train in the distance
rumbles along the tracks
clickety clack clickety clack

Undulating waves caress
the red sandy beach
sun sparkles on the waves
like diamonds

As the sun goes
waves start to gently crash
onto the beach

Happy tails and wet paws
dogs chasing balls in and out of the sea
not a care in the world

Old dogs loping along
young dogs racing over the breakwaters
taking each one
in one stride

Wooden groins once swathed in concrete
stand alone and stark
concrete up ended on beach
with seaweed clinging on

Signs say beware sharp objects
oh what a mess it is
childhood memories are still there
clambering down onto a safe beach

White moon nestles on dark clouds
peeping out through the trees
stars try and come out
give up because of dark clouds

Odd patches blue sky
grey clouds take overhead
trees shake their leaves
swaying unbalanced

Children play
people walk by
cars and lorries roll by
each with a purpose

Clear blue sky
tall blocks of rooms
people chatting
as they walk around

Soft wind gently blows
caresses the water
boats sit in the harbour, oozing money and wealth

Two iron chimneys one giant paddle
great white steamer waiting its turn
Smell of charcoal fish on stick

Hilary Goodman

PRAYERS & THOUGHTS

A THOUGHT FOR ADVENT

Emmanuel, come and give me the strength to make it through this season of gifts and parties.
Keep me focused on you, the greatest gift ever given.

Come into my family and make Yourself at home, let all of us the power you work in our lives and the graces we receive through Your church.

Come open my eyes to the wonders around me. Let my sight be so clear that I always see through the creation to the Creator.

Come and fill me with Your spirit, fill my drooping spirit. Breathe into me the breath of life, that I may soar.

Come to me in moments of great need, keep me, my friends and family safe, and help us to remember that our homes and lives can never fail if we built on You.

Come to me and help me have patience with those around me. Help me to know that I can truly love and understand others because You first loved me.

Come and make known Your will for my life, give me the courage to ask for Your will to be done send the willingness to accept when it is given.

Come to me and make me like a child, open my heart and mind to You and allow me to see with hunger of a newborn and the enthusiasm of a teenager.

Come to me and help me remember that I only succeed in whatever I do because You are there for me guiding, protecting and watching.

The following prayers are taken from the Gideon Bible, which I found comforting during my time in hospital undergoing major back surgery.

Loving Father, help us to discover the destiny for which You are preparing us, the vocation for which we were created.

Anoint us with Your Spirit, so that, whether we are in the wilderness or on the way to Jerusalem we will know Your presence among Your people.

Strengthen us in Your son so that, irrespective of race, colour, creed we may serve You in the least of these Your brothers and sisters.
Amen.

Dear God, You know and understand everything when I feel ill, afraid, lonely, anxious sad or depressed.
Help me to trust You because You love me and promise to be with me always.
Amen.

Dear God, help me to know You are with me in this situation. Take away my fear and reassure me that I have committed my life to You.
You are in control of my circumstances and know what is best for me.
Help me to trust You.
Amen.

A prayer I wrote when I was in my darkest hour:

Lord, when in despair I turn to You, You know my need even before I ask it.
Help me through this difficult phase and bring me the joy of the risen Christ.
You humbled yourself to be born in a lonely manger,
You accepted the gifts of the wise men
even though they foretold Your death.
Help me to be humble and to accept the future whatever it may hold.
Amen.

Throughout all my trials and tribulations, I have found that talking to God as though He were a parent has been so comforting. Below are some prayers that I found helpful.

Strengthen for service, Lord, the hands that have taken Holy things.
May the ears that have heard Your word, be deaf to clamour and dispute.
May the tongues that have sung Your praise, be free from deceit.
May the eyes which have seen the tokens of Your love, shine with the light of hope.
May the bodies which have been fed with Your body, be refreshed with the fullness of your life.
Amen

St Ephraem Syrus (c. 306–373)

Come my light and illumine my darkness,
come my life and revive me from death,
come my physician and heal my wounds,
Come flame of divine love and burn up the thorns of my sins, kindling my heart with the flame of Your love.
Come my King, sit upon the throne of my heart and reign there.
For You alone are my King and my Lord
Amen

Dimitri of Rostov (1709–1757)

Teach me good Lord;
to serve you as You deserve,
to give and not to count the cost,
to fight and not to heed the wounds,
to toil and not to seek for rest,
to labour and not to ask for any reward,
save that of knowing that I do Your will
through Jesus Christ our Lord.
Amen

St Ignatius Loyola (1556–1609)

Lord Jesus Christ
alive and at large in the world,
help me to follow and find You there this week,
in the places where I work
meet people, spend money, and make plans.
Take me as a disciple of Your kingdom.
To see through Your eyes,
and hear the questions You are asking,
to welcome all people with Your trust and truth.
And to change the things that contradict God's love
by the power of the cross
and the freedom of Your Spirit
Amen

Bishop John Taylor (1929–2016)

I arise today
through God's strength to direct me.
God's might to uphold me.
God's wisdom to guide me.
God's eye to look after me.
God's ear to hear me.
God's word to speak to me.
God's hand to guard me.
God's way to be before me.
God's shield to protect me.

Based on St Patrick's Breastplate

A prayer written on the back of a funeral service:

Lord, there are those who are stripped of their garments,
long before it is time for their final rest;
those robbed of health of the body by disease or wasting,
those from whom society has taken all self-worth;
Dementia's children,
whose bodies are sepulchres of minds long since departed.
Help us believe that all they have lost
has already been gathered into Your love.
And that if we too must walk that way
You will never desert us.
Amen

Author unknown

HYMNS & PSALMS

How sweet the name of Jesus sounds
in a believer's ear.
It soothers our sorrows, heals our wounds
and drives away our fear.

It makes the wounded spirit whole
and calms the troubled breast.
'Tis manna to the hungry soul
and to the weary rest.

Dear name the rock on which I build
my shield and hiding place.
My never failing treas'ry filled
with boundless stores of grace.

Jesus my shepherd, brother, friend,
my prophet, priest and King.
My Lord, my life, my way, my end,
accept the praise I bring.

Weak is the effort of my heart
and cold my warmest thought
but when I see Thee as Thou art,
I'll praise Thee as I ought.

Till then I would Thy love proclaim
with every fleeting breath
and may the music of Thy name
refresh my soul in death.

Rev. John Newton (1725–1807)

I heard the voice of Jesu say,
'Come unto me and rest;
lay down, O weary one,
thy head upon my breast.'
I came to Jesus as I was
so weary, worn and sad
I found in Him a resting place
and He has made me glad.

I heard the voice of Jesu say,
'Behold, I freely give
the living water, thirsty one,
stoop down and drink and live.'
I came to Jesus and I drank
of that life-giving stream.
My thirst was quenched, my soul revived
and now I live in Him.

I heard the voice of Jesu say,
'I am this dark world's light.
Look unto me thy morn shall rise
and all thy day be bright.'
I looked to Jesus and I found
in him my star and sun
and in the light of life I'll walk
till travelling days are done.

Horatius Bonar (1808–1889)

Will your anchor hold in the storms of life
when the clouds unfold their wings of strife?
When the strong tides lift and the cables strain
will your anchor drift or firm remain?

*We have an anchor that keeps the soul
steadfast and sure while the billows roll,
fastened to the rock which cannot move
grounded firm and deep in the Saviour's love.*

Will your anchor hold in the straits of fear
when the breakers roar, and the reef is near?
While the surges rage and the wild winds blow
shall the angry waves then your bark o'erflow?

We have an anchor...

Will your anchor hold in the floods of death,
when the waters cold chill your latest breath?
On the rising tide you can never fail
while your anchor hold within the veil.

We have an anchor...

Will your eye behold through the morning light
the city of gold and the harbour bright?
Will you anchor safe by the heavenly shore
when life's storms are past for evermore?

We have an anchor...

Priscilla J Owens (1829–1907)

Eternal Father, strong to save,
Whose arm doth bind the restless wave,
Who bid'st the mighty ocean deep
   its own appointed limits keep;
  O hear us when we cry to thee
   for those in peril on the sea.

O Saviour, whose almighty words
The winds and waves submissive heard,
Who walkedst on the foaming deep,
And calm amid its rage didst sleep:
  O hear us when we cry to thee
   for those in peril on the sea.

O sacred Spirit, who didst brood
  Upon the chaos dark and rude,
Who bad'st its angry tumult cease,
And gavest light and life and peace:
  O hear us when we cry to thee
   for those in peril on the sea.

O Trinity of love and power,
Our brethren shield in danger's hour;
From rock and tempest, fire and foe,
Protect them whereso'er they go:
  And ever let there rise to thee
glad hymns of praise from land and sea.

William Whiting (1825–1878)

Going home, moving on,
through God's open door;
hush, my soul, have no fear,
Christ has gone before.
Parting hurts, love protests,
pain is not denied;
yet, in Christ,
life and hope span the great divide.
Going home, moving on,
through God's open door;
hush, my soul, have no fear,
Christ has gone before,
Christ has gone before.

No more guilt, no more fear,
all the past is healed:
broken dreams now restored,
perfect grace revealed.
Christ has died, Christ is ris'n,
Christ will come again:
death destroyed, life restored,
love shall reign again.
Going home, moving on,
through God's open door;
hush, my soul, have no fear,
Christ has gone before,
Christ has gone before.

Michael Forster (b. 1946)

I have found Taizé chants to be thought-provoking and haunting in their simplicity. Below are just a few of my favourites.

Calm me Lord as you calmed the storm
still me Lord, keep me from harm.
Let all the tumult within me cease.
Enfold me Lord in your peace.

David Adam (1936–2020)

You are the centre; you are my life,
you are the centre, O Lord of my life.
Come Lord and heal me, Lord of my life
Come Lord and teach me, Lord of my life.
You are the centre, Lord of my life.
Give me your Spirit and teach me your ways
Give me your peace Lord and set me free.
You are the centre Lord of my life.

Margaret Rizza (b. 1929)

Extracts from hymns and choruses

Holy, Holy, Holy, Lord God Almighty,
early in the morning, our song shall rise to thee.
Holy, Holy, Holy, merciful and mighty,
God in three persons, Blessed Trinity.

Bishop Christopher Wordsworth (1774–1846)

Dear Lord and Father of mankind
forgive our foolish ways.
Reclothe us in our rightful mind
in purer lives thy service find
in deeper reverence praise
in deeper reverence praise.

John Greenleaf Whittier (1807–1892)

Praise to the Lord, the Almighty, the king of creation
O my soul praise Him for he is thy health and salvation
all ye who hear, now to his temple draw near
Praise him in glad adoration

Joachim Neander (1650–1680)

Amazing grace, how sweet the sound
that saved a wretch like me.
I once was lost but now am found.
Was blind, but now I see.

Rev. John Newton (1725–1807)

Take up thy cross and follow me
I heard the master say.
I gave my life to ransom thee
surrender your all today.
Wherever he leads I'll go
Wherever he leads I'll go.
I'll follow my Christ who loves me
wherever he leads I'll go.

Charles W Everest (1814–1877)

All that I am, all that I do
all that I'll ever have
I offer now to you.
Take and sanctify these gifts
for your honour Lord.
Knowing that I love and serve you is enough reward.
All that I am, all that I do
all that I'll ever have
I offer now to you.

Sebastian Temple (1928–1997)

Lord, make me an instrument of your peace.
Where there is hatred, let me sow love
where there is injury, your pardon
where there is despair, hope
where there is darkness, light
and where there's sadness ever joy.

O master grant that I may never seek so much to be
consoled as to console.
To be understood as to understand
to be loved as to love.
For it is in giving that we receive,
and in pardoning that we are pardoned
and in dying that we are born to eternal life.

St Francis of Assisi (1181–1226)

The following are extracts from Psalms:

Take delight in the Lord
and he will give you the desires of
your heart.

Psalm 37:4

Come let us bow down in worship
let us kneel before the Lord our maker.

Psalm 95:6

Teach us to number our days
that we may gain a heart of wisdom.

Psalm 90:12

Wait for the Lord, be strong and take heart
and wait for the Lord.

Psalm 27:14

Taste and see that Lord is good
Blessed are those who take refuge in him.

Psalm 34:8

Create in me a pure heart, O God,
and renew a steadfast spirit within me.

Psalm 51:10

The Lord is close to the broken hearted and saves those who
are crushed in spirit

Psalm 34:18

A righteous man may have many troubles, but the Lord
delivers him from them all

Psalm 34:19

TALKS

ADVENT SUNDAY

Advent means the arrival or coming of an important person or thing. In our seasonal preparations we can mask the awe inspiring idea that the omnipotent and all powerful God, the creator of the universe and source of all being should choose to come down and be like one of us. Not a chocolate box image or commercial enterprise, but a man. A man who would experience the vulnerability of humankind, homelessness, forced to flee to another country for his life, to face hunger and ultimately to be condemned and die.

Advent is therefore a time of expectancy, a time for watching for the dawn to break from on high. A time when the world's need for Christ becomes clear. Amid our anxieties of debt and society, the need for a saviour has never more expectant.

The challenge for is the Advent is finding the space to think about why it happened in the first place. Let us reflect on the implications of the coming of the Messiah.

Let us look at the Advent calender with fresh eyes, not the here today and gone tomorrow as with the chocolate ones, but focus on the true meaning.

When you open the door on your chocolate calender, spare a thought for those who have no food, shelter, warmth, the simple basics that we accept so readily.

Ours is a world of instant satisfactions and the delay implicit in longing, hoping and waiting is an alien idea. Its more important that Christian s shouldn't compromise the rich themes of Advent by letting Christmas take over too soon.

God grant you
the light of Christmas, which is faith,
the warmth of Christmas, which is love,
the radiance of Christmas, which is purity,
the righteousness of Christmas, which is justice,
the belief in Christmas, which is truth,
the all of Christmas, which is Christ.

DEDICATION SUNDAY

The church then is not just a building. It is a gathering of people, and although each one of us is unique, we are held together by the Spirit of Jesus, who lives within each ones of us, drawing us closer to God and to each other and who enables us to acknowledge Jesus as our Lord.

The church is the people who come together as one people to share in the goodness of God and to celebrate if. Each time we assemble we gather in the warmth of God's love. The little room in which Jesus first appeared has been enlarged to take in the whole world and every age.

Lord Jesus Christ, guide your church in the way that it should go. May we be a healthy body, full of vigour and a proper God-given strength, growing always in your image and carrying your work on earth.

> I dream of a church, where love and people
> are more important than stone and steeple.
>
> I dream of a church, with an open door
> where no-one is privileged except the poor.
>
> I dream of a church, where milk and honey
> will flow more freely, than power and money.
>
> I dream of a church, where young and old
> will be inspired to change the world.
>
> I dream of a church, that will make all
> my dreams come true.

COMMUNION

Just as bread is the visible form of life giving nourishment, so Jesus is the visible form of God's life giving love.

As human beings we need to work together with God our Maker to answer the age-old question:

who am I? and what am I here for?

God has plans for all of us and there are times when we find that the life God calls us is not always easy, and we will find it tiring and hard work. But God will always look after us through these times, leading us and feeding us with whatever strength, energy and rest we need.

If we keep our spiritual eyes and ears open, we will notice the way God looks after us, leads us and feeds us.

Can you see God's love, the way he is interested in the little as well as the big. The way he is generous and loves to give. The way he supports and carries us. The way he is reliable and faithful.

Lord God: What would you like me to see and hear this week? What would you like me to notice? Keep my eyes open and my ears pinned back so that I don't miss you speaking through all the ordinary things of my life.

GOOD NEWS

The Sovereign Lord has filled me with his Spirit and has chosen me to give the good news to the poor. Tell prisoners that they are prisoners no more, tell blind people that they can see, and set the downtrodden free, and go tell everyone the news that the kingdom of God has come, and go tell everyone the news that God's kingdom has come.

This passage is describing Jesus, how? It sounds like the sort of things that he did and would do throughout his earthly ministry.

He was a friend to everyone, from the poor to the rich, the unclean leper to the blind person, even the demons recognized the Son of God. However, no one has ever seen God in the life, but we have plenty of good clues given to us in the writings of the bible. When we are sitting listening to the bible readings or reading the bible ourselves at home, we need to listen, so that when God is speaking to us through his word we are able to hear him.

Jesus came to earth to fulfil the promises of God, wouldn't it be great if and I were as faithful in keeping our promises to God as he is in keeping his promises to us.

Jesus, I know you always speak what is true,
Help me to listen with my heart as well as my ears.
Amen.